Working Together Against

SEXUAL
HARASSMENT

For years, women have kept quiet about sexual harassment, but now they are speaking out and fighting back against their harassers.

❖ THE LIBRARY OF SOCIAL ACTIVISM ❖

Working Together Against

SEXUAL HARASSMENT

Rhoda McFarland

4373

THE ROSEN PUBLISHING GROUP, INC.
NEW YORK

Published in 1996 by The Rosen Publishing Group, Inc.
29 East 21st Street, New York, NY 10010

First Edition

Library of Congress Cataloging-in-Publication Data

McFarland, Rhoda.
    Working together against sexual harassment / by Rhoda McFarland.
      p.   cm. — (The library of social activism)
    Includes bibliographical references and index.
    Summary: Examines sexual harassment in school and the workplace and discusses ways to become involved locally and nationally to stop its occurrence.
    ISBN 0-8239-1775-4
    1. Sexual harassment of women—United States—Juvenile literature. 2. Sexism—United States—Juvenile literature. [1. Sexual harassment.] I. Title. II. Series.
HQ1237.5.U6M34   1996
305.42′8973—dc20   96-14434
                                                      CIP
                                                      AC

Manufactured in the United States of America

Contents

INTRODUCTION

IN SEPTEMBER 1992, *SEVENTEEN* MAGAZINE conducted a survey of its readers about sexual harassment at school. More than 4,000 teenage girls from all over the United States responded. The survey showed that 97 percent of the time, the harassers were boys at school. In most of the schools, no action was taken when the harassment was reported to a teacher or an administrator. The usual reaction to such reports was, "Boys will be boys," or "It's just something boys do; ignore it."

Schools can no longer ignore sexual harassment. Action must be taken to protect students. By federal law, schools must provide an education for students in an environment free of sexual harassment. People must be educated about sexual harassment so that everyone can be provided with a harassment-free environment at school and at work.

The first part of this book tells about

women's long struggle against sexism and sexual harassment. It tells of the fight for equal rights. It explains exactly what sexual harassment is. The second part of the book tells you how to get together with others to work against sexism and sexual harassment.

You have a right to go to school without being harassed or discriminated against. You have a right to work in an environment free from sexism and harassment. You have a right to make choices and have opportunities based on your interests and abilities, not your sex. Claiming those rights for yourself can be difficult without help. The old saying, "There's strength in numbers," is what this book is all about. Claim your rights by getting involved and working together with others.

❖ **QUESTIONS TO ASK YOURSELF** ❖

In this book we will explore the problem of sexual harassment and try to explain why it exists and what you can do to help stop the problem. 1) Do you know what sexual harassment is? 2) Does your school or workplace have a policy concerning sexual harassment? 3) If yes, what is the policy? If no, would you be willing to work to make one?

Some guys think they are complimenting a girl when they stare
and make comments, but in fact, many girls feel insulted.

chapter

1

BECOMING AWARE

"I AM SICK OF THE FILTHY BOYS IN THIS school!" Sharon snarled as she threw her books on her desk. *"I would like to walk down the hall just once without some creep mooing when I walk by."*

"They're just having a little fun, Sharon. What's the matter, can't you take it?" This came from Ronnie Clark.

"Harassment is not my idea of fun," Sharon said.

"Aw, come on. Harassment?" cried Ronnie.

"Actually, Sharon's right," said Mr. Lee, their American Problems teacher. "Women have been the victims of harassment for a very long time. Many women are no longer willing to accept that kind of treatment. Many women are following in the footsteps of Anita Hill and fighting back against their harassers.

"I had planned to bring up sexual harassment and sexism as a problem for us to look into later in the term. Since it has come up, now seems like a good time to talk about it," said Mr. Lee. He began

his class by discussing the Clarence Thomas nomination and the Tailhook Naval Convention.

❖ RECENT CASES OF HARASSMENT ❖

In 1991, Clarence Thomas was nominated as a Supreme Court Justice. Before his nomination was approved by the Senate, Anita Hill, a professor at the University of Oklahoma, came forward and accused him of sexual harassment. Sexual harassment is any unwanted or unwelcome sexual behavior toward another person. She said that the harassment had occurred while she worked with Thomas at the Equal Employment Opportunity Commission (EEOC) in the early 1980s. She claimed that Thomas, then her boss, regularly made sexual comments to her and talked about pornographic movies he saw. She said that these behaviors made her feel uncomfortable. Thomas denied Hill's charges.

The Thomas confirmation hearings divided the country. In a poll done by the *Wall Street Journal/NBC News* in 1991, 24 percent of the people believed Hill while 40 percent believed Thomas. In a close vote, the Senate voted to approve Thomas's nomination to the Supreme Court. A year later, the public's opinion reversed: 44 percent believed Hill and only 34 percent believed Thomas.

In the past, women kept silent about harassment for many reasons: they were afraid that no

Anita Hill helped bring greater national attention to the problem of sexual harassment.

one would believe them, they would not get raises or promotions, or they might lose their jobs. But when Anita Hill decided to go public with her story, she created a greater awareness of the problem. She gave courage to many other women to speak out against their harassers. According to the EEOC, almost 10,000 harassment complaints were filed in 1992. That was an increase of 6,000 as compared to 1980, and 4,000 more than were filed in 1991. Women who have been harassed by male government officials are speaking out in record numbers. Harassment claims forced Senator Brock Adams of Washington to retire in 1992. More than twenty female employees of Senator Robert Packwood filed charges against him for unwanted sexual advances. According to one woman, the harassment went as far back as 1969. The senator resigned.

In the military, harassment of female personnel was largely ignored until 1991, when one woman decided to speak out. The Navy investigated three complaints of harassment of female Navy personnel by male pilots at the 1991 Tailhook Convention. After a two-year investigation, there was still no conviction. Of the hundreds of men reportedly involved, only two were arrested. Charges against them were eventually dropped. Thirty-five high-ranking officers were at the convention. All of them claimed they

Janet Reno became the first woman Attorney General in United States history.

knew nothing about the harassment. On the news magazine *60 Minutes*, one naval officer said he had stood next to Admiral Frank B. Kelso, then Chief of Naval Operations. The pilot said that Kelso said nothing about what was happening—giving his silent approval. Even though no high-ranking officers were punished, the sexual harassment at the Tailhook Convention was not repeated at later conventions.

❖ CONTINUING PROGRESS ❖

Although the United States still has a long way to go before there is true equality between the sexes, progress has been made. The year 1992 was called "Year of the Woman" because a

record six women were members of the Senate and forty-seven were members of the House of Representatives. Although this was the largest number of women ever to serve in the two houses of Congress, women still make up only six percent of the Senate and ten percent of the House.

According to the *National Law Journal*, only 2,828 of the 25,382 law partners in the nation's largest firms are women. And according to the American Medical Association, only 3,465 of the 69,407 surgeons are women. The National Federation of Press Women reported that of 1,581 publishers of daily newspapers, only 119 are women.

When Mr. Lee finished speaking, Sharon said, "Men are in a position of power in society; they control the money, the government, and the ability to shape public opinion. It's a power that many men are not willing to let go."

"Even the boys in school say things to us to make themselves feel big," said Laura. "When they make comments about me, I feel put down and powerless."

"That's dumb," Ronnie said. "Guys are just having fun."

"Why do you think Anita Hill waited ten years to say something?" Wendy asked.

"What about the women who worked for Senator Packwood? One woman said he harassed her in

1969," Sharon said. "That was over twenty years ago."

"Who would they have complained to, anyway?" asked Mike.

Mr. Lee explained, "Title VII of the Civil Rights Act of 1964 says that discrimination on the basis of race, color, religion, national origin, or sex is unlawful. Sexual harassment comes under sex discrimination. The law has been in the books a long time. Complaints can be made to the EEOC. However, the first step in making a complaint is usually within the company you work for. There's supposed to be company policy set up for harassment complaints."

"So if someone complains, the boss finds out about it right away," Mike said. "So most of the time a woman doesn't complain because she's afraid of losing her job."

"Or afraid she'll be accused of having come on to the guy," Wendy added.

"Think about what we've said today, and we'll continue this tomorrow," said Mr. Lee when the bell rang.

❖ QUESTIONS TO ASK YOURSELF ❖

Sexual harassment is a serious concern, especially among women. 1) Have you ever been sexually harassed? 2) Did you report it? What was the result? 3) If you didn't, why didn't you?

chapter

2

THE ROOTS OF SEXISM

"*I'VE THOUGHT ABOUT WHAT WE DISCUSSED yesterday,*" *Ronnie said in class the next day.* "*I can see what you mean. You know, about men in the government and running big companies. But isn't that just the way it has always been?*"

"*Just because it has always been that way doesn't mean it's right,*" *Karen said.* "*Women want you to look at the way things have been for them and to realize that they may need to change.*"

"*Not everybody wants things changed,*" *said Mike.*

"*Of course, most men don't want change. They're the ones in power,*" *Wendy said, glaring.*

"*Some women don't want change either,*" *said Sharon.* "*My mom and I talked about it last night. She said that she learned in church that women are supposed to obey their husbands. There are a lot of women who believe that.*"

"*That's true, Sharon,*" *Mr. Lee agreed.* "*Some women think that women need to be at home, taking care of their families while their husbands provide for*

Women in North America have come a long way from the days when they were legally considered the property of their husbands or fathers. Women have taken charge of their own lives and become their own bosses.

*the family. They feel that men should be the heads of
the house. They don't agree with women who want
equal rights." Mr. Lee went on to explain the history
of sexism.*

❖ EXAMINING SEXISM ❖

In many societies, men have always dominat-
ed. When the Constitution of the United States
was written, women and slaves were not given
the right to vote. Women also had no rights of
ownership. As a matter of fact, English law
allowed husbands to own their wives. In 1868,
the Fourteenth Amendment freed the slaves and
gave male blacks the right to vote. But it took
more than a fifty-year struggle before women
were given the same right. It was the same in
many parts of the world. In Greece about 2,500
years ago, women had the same rights as slaves.
In ancient Rome, women were under their husband's rule. Even today, women in parts of
Central and South America, Africa, and Asia are
not allowed to own property. In fact, in many
cultures girls and women are still the property of
their husbands or fathers.

Some religions throughout the world have
taught that men are better than women. The
Hindu Code says that a woman must be under a
man's control. The Confucian Marriage Manual
tells a woman to distrust herself and obey her
husband. Muslim women in some societies are

still required to cover their faces and wear long, loose robes.

A man's work has often been viewed as being more important than a woman's. In ancient times there were celebrations when the men brought home the meat they killed. This is understandable because they risked their lives to get the meat. However, it was the women who gathered or grew most of the food.

Even today, men's work is often valued above that of women. This may be because women who are homemakers or care for their children do not earn money.

Even when women work outside the home, their jobs are sometimes considered less important than their husbands'. Many families move because the father is transferred or gets a better job. When a couple wants to start a family, it is often the woman who is expected to give up her job to take care of the children.

Sometimes women seem to "disappear" after they get married. A recent news story about the number of men dying of AIDS (acquired immunodeficiency syndrome) in Africa illustrates this. Under a picture of children, the caption said that these were orphans whose fathers had died of AIDS. What happened to their mothers? "Orphan" means not having any parents, no father *or* mother. In this story, the mothers of the children weren't mentioned.

Women in countries all over the world are regularly beaten by their husbands. Uganda has laws against wife-beating, but few of the women can read or write. Many do not know about the laws. Women in Peru got tired of beatings. In some Peruvian towns, women carry whistles to blow when they are attacked or beaten. The sound of a whistle brings a crowd of women to defend the one being attacked.

During wars, raping females was considered to be part of defeating the enemy. Rape is a form of violence in which a man tries to control and shame the victim. Rape is also seen as a way to humiliate another man. To rape someone's wife or daughter may be seen in the same way as violating a man's home.

❖ **CHANGING IDEAS** ❖

In many societies men have long been in the position of power, and women have been relatively powerless—powerless at home, at work, at school, and in relationships. Today many women are not willing to accept that powerlessness. They are no longer accepting the traditional roles of "housewife" or "mother." Women do not want to be told what they can and can't do. They want to make their own career choices rather than have society choose for them. They are demanding to use their intelligence and abilities. They are demanding to be heard and taken

Hillary Clinton has played a more obvious policy making role in her husband's presidency than any other First Lady.

seriously. They are refusing to be limited because of their gender.

When Bill Clinton, the president of the United States, married his wife Hillary, she didn't take his last name. She was Hillary Rodham until Clinton ran for governor of Arkansas. Clinton's campaign advisers thought voters might not vote for a man whose wife didn't use his name. To some people, it meant that he didn't have much control over his wife. At the beginning of the presidential campaign, Clinton said that the office would be a partnership: vote for one and get two. Hillary Rodham Clinton was very much a part of his campaign,

speaking out and giving her opinions. When his advisers sensed that some voters didn't like the idea of a partnership that included Clinton's wife involved in the running of the country, she suddenly stopped speaking out. She took a backseat and no longer had a major role in Clinton's campaign.

❖ **QUESTIONS TO ASK YOURSELF** ❖

In most societies throughout human history, women have been second-class citizens. 1) Do you think that is right? 2) How are girls treated in your circle of friends? 3) Do you think improvements are needed at your school?

chapter

3

THE FIGHT FOR RIGHTS

*"**THE** **FIGHT** **FOR** **EQUAL** **RIGHTS** **FOR** **WOMEN** has been going on for a long time," Mr. Lee told the class. "In the United States it started as early as when the Constitution was written, but it was often a difficult fight, especially for early leaders of women's rights."*

❖ EARLY LEADERS FOR WOMEN'S RIGHTS ❖

When the movement for equal rights for women started in the United States, it was met with opposition and ridicule. Many clergymen went as far as to say that equality for women was against the will of God. Women who protested for equality were considered unfeminine and were called the "shrieking sisterhood." When feminist leaders went on tours to speak in support of women's rights, they were threatened with physical violence. Meetings were often stormed by protesters. Some important leaders in the movement included Susan B. Anthony,

Dr. Elizabeth Blackwell (the first woman to receive a medical degree), Antoinette Brown (the first woman minister in the United States), and Lucretia Coffin Mott.

Women didn't always fight alone; there were many men who supported equality. Even in colonial America, many groups, such as the Religious Society of Friends (Quakers), and many individuals, including writer Thomas Paine, supported equal rights for women. However, some men supported one right but not others. Some may have wanted to give women the right to vote, but they didn't want women to hold government office.

Although many women fought hard to gain an equal status with men, it did not mean they were against men. As a matter of fact, many feminist leaders, including Blackwell, Lucy Stone, and Catherine Waugh McCullough, married men who supported them and their work.

❖ THE STRUGGLE ABROAD ❖

Women all over the world have been fighting for equal rights for a long time. In her book *Sisterhood Is Global*, Robin Morgan tells the "herstory" of countries around the world. In 1823, a group of women in Argentina organized to protest laws that discriminated against women. In Denmark, the Women's Social Union was started in the mid-1800s to develop trade

unions for women. In 1898, the Danish
Women's Suffrage Committee began fighting for
women's right to vote, and in 1915, all citizens
over twenty-one got the right to vote. Women in
Finland won voting rights in 1906.

French women began their fight for rights
very early. In 1164, Héloïse founded a religious
community of learning for women. In 1339,
Christine De Pesan wrote what is considered to
be the first feminist tract. In 1754, Madeleine de
Scudéry and Marie de Gourney wrote in
defense of women's rights in the *Ladies' Journal*.
Olympe de Gouges was beheaded after she
wrote "The Declaration of Women's Rights" in
1790.

In Japan, education for women started in
1872. By 1876, the Women's Normal School
opened to train women to be primary teachers.
The Peace and Preservation Law of 1889
prevented women from participating in political
parties, but Kishida Toshiko campaigned for
women's voting rights anyway.

❖ PROGRESS IN THE UNITED STATES ❖

In the United States, women gained the right
to vote in 1920. But some of the greatest
progress in gaining entry to education, political
rights, and jobs happened during World War II.
During the war, women entered the workforce
in great numbers. With many of the men gone

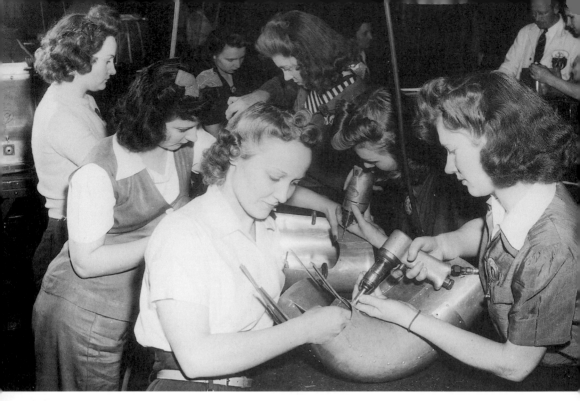

During World War II, when many of the men went to war, American women first entered the work force in great numbers.

because of the war, women kept the country running. They discovered that they could do the work as well as, if not better than men.

When the men came back at the end of the war and reclaimed their jobs, some women stayed with their new-found jobs. The country resumed normal activities, and the economy boomed. Wages improved for men, but women were still paid less than men for the same work. This unfairness made women angry. Trade unions helped women in industry receive fairer pay. However, women were not usually promoted to the higher-paying jobs of supervisors or managers.

Another important factor in the women's movement occurred when the men came back from the war. The economy was good, and many couples began having children. The "Baby Boom" was under way. Some time later so was the "Divorce Boom." More women than ever before had to support themselves and their children alone. They wanted and needed better-paying jobs. More women than ever before went to college. They entered the professions. However, they usually could not get jobs as managers and higher-level executives. Women were as well qualified as men, maybe better, but men were still chosen for promotions ahead of them.

Women got tired of the discrimination. They did something constructive with their anger. They joined together to fight for their rights. They spoke out, and the media (newspapers, radio, and television) carried their message across the country. They were able to reach more people than ever before. The National Organization for Women (NOW) was founded in 1966. The first national organization of its kind, NOW became the symbol of the women's movement. Six years later, *Ms.* magazine was founded. It was the first women's magazine that didn't focus on women as homemakers and mothers.

Progress toward equal rights for women has been slow. Among many women's organizations today, NOW still stands out with the largest

Ms. magazine was the first women's magazine that didn't focus on women as homemakers or mothers.

membership throughout the United States. Its members are women and men who support full equality for women. They want to end prejudice and discrimination against women in government, industry, the professions, politics, education, labor unions, science, medicine, the law, the courts, religion, and all fields of importance in society.

The National Women's Political Caucus (NWPC) is the second-largest women's group. The NWPC focuses on gaining greater political influence for women. It raises political issues in elections; it wants women in policy-making positions in political parties. It also supports women

candidates and men who support women's issues.

Joining together, women have brought their issues into the open. Women in the '90s are demanding more respect. They are speaking out for their rights. Harassment in the military, in government, in schools, and in the workplace is no longer being ignored. Sexism that was once endured out of fear or embarrassment is being talked about. The women's movement has changed the social climate to allow women of all ages to speak out.

As the class ended, Sharon spoke up. "I'm speaking out too. I'm tired of being harassed, and I'm going to do something about it."

"I'm with you, Sharon," said Wendy. "Let's get together and see what we can do."

"Anyone else who's tired of the harassment can join us," Sharon invited.

❖ **QUESTIONS TO ASK YOURSELF** ❖

The fight for women's rights has been going on for centuries. 1) Have you read biographies of some of the famous early feminist leaders? 2) When did women secure the right to vote in this country? 3) How did women's gaining the right to vote improve opportunities for women?

chapter

4

WHAT IS HARASSMENT?

"THE GIRLS ARE SURE MAKING A LOT OUT OF this," Brian said to Mike and Ronnie at lunch.

"Yeah," Mike agreed. "Luisa told me she felt uncomfortable when I stood so close to her in the hall. Can you believe that?"

"I don't know what to do anymore," Brian said. "I'm not sure what's harassment and what's okay."

"Well, all this started in Mr. Lee's class. Let's ask him about it," Ronnie suggested.

Mr. Lee was pleased when the boys talked with him. He said they had a good point. He asked the class to do some research at the library. Then they discussed in class what they discovered.

❖ WHAT IS SEXUAL HARASSMENT? ❖

Sexual harassment is any unwanted and unwelcome sexual behavior toward another person. Federal law protects males as well as females. At school, harassment includes any unwelcome sexual advances or requests for sexual favors.

Unwanted and unwelcome touching, and standing too close, are some
sexually harassing behaviors.

Anything that is said or done or that creates an
"intimidating or hostile" environment that
affects a student's education can be considered
harassment.

According to a 1992 study by the American
Association of University Women, sexual harassment is any unwanted conduct that interferes
with your life. Mike wasn't harassing Luisa
because he stood close to her one time in the
hall. But if he continues after she tells him she
feels uncomfortable, then it might be considered
harassment. The behavior must interfere with
Luisa's life in some way. For example, she may
decide to go into the classroom when she sees

Mike coming down the hall. If her decision to change her usual behavior of standing in the hall and talking to friends is based on avoiding Mike in the hall, then his behavior is harassment. He has interfered with her life.

❖ HOW DO I KNOW IT'S HARASSMENT? ❖

You may be confused, like Brian, about what exactly is harassment. People have different ideas of what is considered harassment. For example, one girl may not mind if a boy says to her, "Do you look good today!" But if he says the same thing to another girl, she may deck him. Sometimes it can be hard to tell if comments and behaviors are wanted or unwanted.

Here are some questions you can ask yourself that can help you decide if a behavior is harassment.

- Would you want your comments to be heard by your friends and family?
- Would you want someone to say or do this to your mother, sister, girlfriend, father, brother, boyfriend?
- Do you have some kind of power over this person? Are you bigger, older, more popular, someone whose approval he or she wants? Are you the boyfriend or girlfriend whom the person wants to please? Are you a manager, teacher, older relative?

- Has the person told you that he or she does not like what you are doing or saying?
- Do you laugh at the person's discomfort when you say something sexual?

Most girls do like to receive a compliment on how they look. But they don't want a boy staring at the front of their blouse while he compliments them. They don't want him to pat their behinds or trap them at their lockers.

The following are examples of sexually harassing behaviors:

- Touching or grabbing in a sexual way
- Cornering or standing too close
- Sexual notes or pictures
- Sexual gestures, comments, jokes
- Pressure for or forced sexual activity
- Asking someone out over and over after being refused
- Telephoning repeatedly when asked not to
- Making kissing sounds or other noises with the mouth, name-calling
- Obscene t-shirts, hats, pins
- Spreading sexual rumors
- Bra-snapping, flashing, or mooning
- Rating someone's sexual desirability
- Writing something sexual about someone on a wall or door

❖ **MALES AND FEMALES VIEW BEHAVIOR** ❖
DIFFERENTLY

One thousand men and women in Los Angeles were asked how they would feel if someone asked them to have sex. Sixty-seven percent of the men said they would feel complimented. Only 17 percent of the women considered it a compliment. What might seem positive or not important to one person may be disliked by or upsetting to another.

Male harassers often believe that their behavior makes them sexually attractive. In fact, most females think the behavior is a turn-off.

Because of these different viewpoints, it is easy to see how misunderstandings can happen. It is important for males and females to talk about behaviors that might be harassment. To stop harassment at school, young people must speak out. Ignoring a problem will not make it go away. You can speak to your parents, teachers, or religious leaders about your concerns.

Most of the time, however, harassment is ignored. Teenagers being harassed don't want to cause trouble. They fear being laughed at. They are afraid others will think they are making a big deal out of nothing. They don't want to be blamed for causing the harassment.

Often behavior that feels like harassment to one person is thought to be flirting by another.

You can look in your local library for more information about harassment.

The following are some ways to know the difference between flirting and harassment.

Sexual Harassment	*Flirting*
Makes you feel bad, sad, ugly, angry, powerless	Makes you feel good, happy, attractive, in control
Takes away self-esteem	Adds to self-esteem
Puts you down	Is a compliment
May be frightening	Never frightens

❖ AWARENESS IS THE BEGINNING ❖ OF CHANGE

Groups like NOW work to bring awareness of sexual harassment and sexism to our society. Members work together to bring about change. You can become a part of that effort to end inequality of the sexes. You can join others to fight against sexual harassment and sexism.

❖ QUESTIONS TO ASK YOURSELF ❖

Many people claim that they don't know what sexual harassment is. 1) Do you have specific ideas on the subject? 2) Have you ever told someone to stop harassing you? 3) If so, did that person take your request seriously or try to make a joke of it?

chapter

5

WORKING TOGETHER AT SCHOOL

EIGHT GIRLS AND THREE BOYS MET AT Sharon's house that evening. The girls were surprised to see Brian, Mike, and Ronnie and asked why the boys had decided to come to the meeting.

Brian said, "I just realized that Amy Winters has been harassing me all year. I'm tired of her pinching my behind every time she gets near me. I'm willing to work to stop harassment at school."

"Great! I'm glad you guys are here," Wendy said. Then she said to everyone, "I don't want to just sit around and talk about this stuff. I want to do something about it."

"So do I," said Sharon. "That's why I wanted to get a group together. Mr. Lee said it is when people work together that things begin to change."

"Do you suppose NOW could help us do something here?" asked Laura. "They're all over the United States. I can contact them for more information. There's a group here."

"I know NOW is interested in stopping sexual

If harassment is a problem in your school, you can work together with your friends to find solutions to solve the problem.

harassment at school. I remember reading an article about it in a magazine," Liz said.

"First we need to find out if there's a sexual harassment policy at school. If there isn't a policy, maybe we could do something about getting one," said Sharon.

What Sharon and her friends decided to do is important. They see that sexual harassment is a problem in their school, and they are willing to do something about it. Sexual harassment is a big problem in many schools. It's important that students take an active role in the fight to end it. If you see a problem, or if you or your friends are the victims of harassment, tell someone.

Voice your concern to a teacher or an administrator. Get your parents and friends involved. Everyone has the right to go to school and learn in an environment free of harassment.

The first step is to determine if your school has a sexual harassment policy.

❖ SCHOOL POLICY ❖

School districts are concerned about sexual harassment. Under Title IX of the 1979 Education Act, a school system can lose all its funds from the federal government if it discriminates on the basis of sex. Allowing sexual harassment is considered sexual discrimination.

Districts all over the United States are developing harassment policies to protect themselves. Students and their parents may file a complaint with the federal government if they feel their school permits harassment.

❖ TAKING STEPS TO ESTABLISH ❖ A POLICY

Get an adult to help. It is always best to have an adult's support. Concerned parents or teachers make strong supporters. An adult can get the attention of school officials more easily than a student. An adult can also suggest how you can best go about getting the attention you need. Let the adult open as many doors as possible for you.

If there is a policy in your school, find out:

- how teachers, other school staff, students, and parents are made aware of it
- what behaviors are considered harassment
- what steps to follow if you are harassed
- what will happen to the student harasser or the adult (administrator, teacher, staff) harasser
- what will happen to the adult (administrator, teacher, staff) who is aware of sexual harassment but does not report it
- what help is offered for victims of sexual harassment
- how the complaint will be investigated; will it be confidential; who will investigate?

If no policy exists, take steps to put one in place. Write a letter to the superintendent of the school district. If your district is working on a policy, offer to help. Student input may be needed.

If there are no plans for a policy, take action to put one in place. Ask to speak at the next board meeting and student council meeting. Be prepared. Plan what you are going to say. Take a support person with you, or have someone else speak to support you. Work together to present the issue in a positive way to gain support. You can even ask your principal for help.

Explain how the issue of sexual harassment fits into existing school policy. Most policies

If your school doesn't have a sexual harassment policy, you can talk to teachers and administrators about setting one up.

have a statement about the school's responsibility for students and also a section on student rights. For example: "Every school is responsible for providing a safe learning environment. Every student also has the right to be treated with respect." A statement about harassment would fit under a safe learning environment or as a part of student rights.

Follow the school board's handling of the issue. Talk to other students, teachers, and parents of your friends. Your group needs to be at the next meeting when the issue is discussed. Get as many adults as possible to attend.

Write thank you letters to the school boards,

the superintendent, the principal, other students, and all the other adults who helped you. People are more likely to help next time when they know they are appreciated this time.

❖ DEVELOPING A POLICY ❖

If your school district is just starting to develop a policy on sexual harassment, it may take several months before it is completed. Be patient, be helpful, and be positive.

Getting a policy on sexual harassment will not bring harassment to an end. It is just the beginning. Changing behavior takes time. Some people will not take the policy seriously. Others will choose not to follow it. Students have to be taught to speak up if they are harassed or if they know of other students who are being harassed. Your job is not over when you have a policy. Your leadership is needed to create the positive change you want in your school.

❖ QUESTIONS TO ASK YOURSELF ❖

Schools are beginning to take sexual harassment seriously and adopt policies about it.
1) Does your school have such a policy?
2) Do the students respect it? 3) What happens to a student who harasses another?

chapter

6

WORKING TOGETHER LOCALLY AND NATIONALLY

*A FEW DAYS AFTER THE MEETING, LAURA SENT
a letter to the National Organization for Women.
One day when she came home from school, she
found a letter from NOW on the counter. Laura ran
to call Karen to tell her about the letter.*

*"Wow! That's great. So what are you planning to
do?" Karen asked.*

*"Well, I need to sit down and look at our choices.
After I understand what they are, we can all get
together and decide what we want to do," Laura
answered. "Let's talk to everybody and set a time.
The letter says the NOW president in the state can tell
me how we can start a separate chapter. Maybe I'll
call her and ask her to send us the information
about that."*

*"I'll leave the research up to you," Karen said.
"I'll contact the others. As soon as you're ready, we
can set up the meeting."*

❖ CONTACTING A NATIONAL ❖ ORGANIZATION

Writing or calling a national organization for information is a good way to find out about the group. If you do not know the address, you can find it at your local library. Go to the reference section and ask for *The Encyclopedia of Associations*. The librarian will show you how to use it. Thousands of organizations are listed there. Each listing gives the address, telephone number, and name of the president or executive officer. There is also a short paragraph describing the organization. In addition, see the organizations listed on page 61 of this book.

Check the phone book to see if there is a local group of the organization you are interested in. In smaller towns with weekly newspapers, meetings of organizations are often listed in the paper. Your local organization can give you information.

❖ THE NATIONAL ORGANIZATION ❖ FOR WOMEN (NOW)

The National Organization for Women (NOW) is one of the most powerful organizations working for equality and an end to sexual harassment. NOW believes that women should have an equal place in every field of importance in American society.

You can contact a national women's organization for information or for ideas of starting your own organization.

❖ STARTING A NOW GROUP ❖

Each state has a NOW president. The state president has information for starting a group. Your local NOW chapter can give you the address and telephone number of your state president. You can also write or call the national office.

Starting your own chapter of NOW can be complicated. Chapters have responsibilities to the state and national organizations. It is hard for groups in schools to meet those responsibilities. But there is a much easier way to become a group of your own.

❖ BECOMING AN ACTION TEAM ❖

An action team works with the local NOW

chapter. Under the local chapter, the action team decides what issues it wants to address. The team sets up its own meetings and elects its own officers. All dues are paid to the local chapter. Action teams can have someone from the local NOW chapter act as an adviser. When a local, state, or national activity is coming up, the action team is called on to participate. The action team can also ask the local chapter for support on their projects.

Sometimes school groups run into problems because their leaders graduate. NOW likes to see young women work with the local chapter through action teams. The local chapter can give leadership training. When action team leaders graduate, new leaders can be trained to take over.

Some states have a Young Feminist Adviser. She keeps in touch with the action teams in the state. She advises them and calls them when their support is needed for an event. Many colleges have action teams. The state Young Feminist Adviser helps organize the teams. She acts as a link between the action team and the national organization.

Most NOW chapters are eager to have young women join them. If there is no local group in your town, contact the national NOW office in Washington, DC. Ask to be put in touch with someone who can help you organize an action team.

❖ TAKE ACTION ❖

You can make a difference. You understand how sexual harassment and sexism degrade a person. You can make others aware of sexist, harassing behavior. Others in your school and community may not even be aware of the problem, or if they are, they may not know what to do about it. You need to get your message across to as many people as you can. If your school has a newspaper or a radio station, you can write an editorial in the paper or get some airtime at the station to spread your message.

❖ QUESTIONS TO ASK YOURSELF ❖

National organizations are glad to work with young people on special problems. 1) Does your community have a chapter of NOW? 2) Does your school have an active group working against sexual harassment? 3) What other organizations in your community are working to promote equal rights?

chapter

7

WORKING TOGETHER POLITICALLY

AT LUNCH A FEW DAYS LATER, EVERYONE talked about what they had learned in class about another women's organization called the National Women's Political Caucus. "I like the idea that the NWPC supports women of different political parties," Laura said.

"They also teach women candidates how to run their campaigns," Brian said.

"Are we going to find out if there's a group near here?" Sharon asked.

"We're thinking about it," Laura answered. "It says, 'When women stay out of politics they give others the right to make choices for them.' I want to get involved. I want to have something to say about who represents me and makes choices for me."

❖ THE NATIONAL WOMEN'S ❖ POLITICAL CAUCUS (NWPC)

Working with the National Women's Political Caucus (NWPC) is an important way of working toward political equality and the ending of

The National Women's Political Caucus encourages young women to become more active in politics.

sexual harassment. The NWPC is dedicated to getting women elected and appointed to political office. They believe that women are not equally represented in government. The NWPC thinks women must be on the "inside" of government for women's issues to get the full attention and respect they deserve.

The goal of the NWPC is political equality. The NWPC, also referred to as the Caucus, believes that women deserve equal opportunities in the political process. It believes in equality in all public leadership positions. It wants to see women in all elected offices: on school boards and county commissions, in city hall and the state legislature, in the United States Congress and the White House.

❖ ACTIVITIES OF THE CAUCUS ❖

You can get involved in the NWPC. The NWPC trains women on how to get elected. They train political campaign workers to organize. They teach them how to raise funds for the candidate and how to get people out to vote.

The NWPC supports a program that encourages more young people to become involved in government. College students can become paid interns to work with state and national lawmakers. Political science departments in colleges and universities have information about internships. You can find out what political opportunities are

available to young women in your state by contacting your state's Commission on the Status of Women.

❖ GETTING INVOLVED ❖

By working locally, you can support candidates for state and national office. In 1992, four women were elected to the 100-member U.S. Senate, bringing the total to six. Twenty-four women were elected to the House of Representatives, making a total of forty-seven women in the 435-member House. That's progress, but it is a long way from equal political representation for women.

The NWPC recommends that you get involved right at home in local elections. Women who are running for office need your help. Candidates elected to city and county office often go on to run for state office. Many state officials run for the U.S. House and Senate. It is important for women to be elected to local offices. These open the way to state and national offices in the future. You can become an important part of this by becoming a volunteer for someone in your town or city.

Go to the campaign headquarters of the candidate you support and offer to help. You do not have to be old enough to vote to help. There are many jobs to do around a campaign office.

Help get voters to the polls. To vote, one

must be a registered voter. You may be able to help register people to vote. In most states, when you are eighteen, you can register people to vote.

The NWPC is making a big push to get younger women involved. They are working on getting Caucuses on college and university campuses. If you live near a college or university, see if there is a Young Women's Political Caucus on campus. You will be welcomed in their group. They may even work with you to get a group started in your school.

Contact the NWPC and ask for information (see page 61). Materials sent to you will include the name of the head of your state's Caucus. You can write or call her for more detailed information about Caucus activities and opportunities in your area. Get involved and help in the fight against sexism. You can make a difference.

❖ QUESTIONS TO ASK YOURSELF ❖

Women are making a difference in the political field. 1) Does your community have a chapter of NWPC? 2) Do you find politics and elections interesting? 3) Could you organize a school group to work with NWPC?

chapter

8

HOW TO MAKE A DIFFERENCE

AS THE SCHOOL YEAR ENDED, MR. LEE AND
the class talked of the high points of their year
together. "You should be proud of yourselves for being
the push behind creating the new sexual harassment
policy here at school. Working together with the
Student Council and then the District School Board
was very effective. Your committee of both sexes
impressed everyone. You deserve a lot of credit for the
way you handled the entire project," said Mr. Lee.

"I was so scared when I had to speak at those
meetings, but it was worth it," Sharon said. "I can
walk down the hall knowing I won't hear all the
noises and wisecracks. It's great."

Laura said she was glad the subject of harass-
ment had come up. That's how she got involved with
NOW. She could work against harassment and all
kinds of sexual discrimination. She said, "There's so
much to be done. I'll have something to work for
and a group to work with."

"And Wendy and I are helping to get Janet

*Green elected to the County Commission and
Michael Edwards to the School Board," added Kim.*

*"I'll be helping to register people to vote," said
Ronnie.*

*"I'm really proud of the way you've taken
action," Mr. Lee told the class.*

❖ GETTING TOGETHER AGAINST . . . ❖

The struggle against harassment and sexism is
far from over. In the United States, we are making progress. Sexist, harassing behavior is not as
readily accepted or overlooked as it was in the
past. However, it still goes on every day. Women
have quit jobs to get away from harassers. Those
who can't afford to quit their jobs live in fear of
losing them if they make an issue of the harassment. Women of all ages still live with sexual
remarks from men rather than confronting that
kind of harassment. Shyness, fear, and not
knowing what to do keep teens from reporting
harassment.

Every time harassment is ignored, it gives the
harasser permission to continue. Confronting
harassment alone is scary and can be very
difficult. But you can get together with others
to work against sexual harassment and
sexism.

❖ TAKE ACTION ❖

Personally. If you are personally harassed, it is

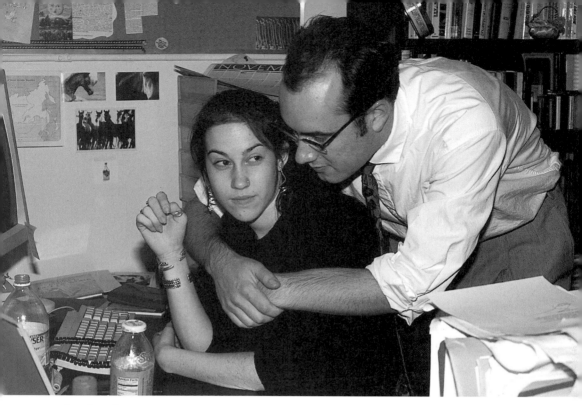

Confronting your harasser may be frightening, but ignoring the harassment gives the harasser permission to continue.

important to confront your harasser safely. Here are the steps to do that.

- Follow your school's policy or, if the harassment occurs at work, the policy at your company.
- If there is no policy, tell the harasser how you feel when you are harassed. Then tell him or her to stop.
- If it happens again, report it to someone in authority. Write down what happened and give it to the person to whom you report.
- If the harassment continues after you report it, go to someone higher in authority. Some higher authorities are: your local School

Board, the State Department of Education, the Office of Civil Rights, the Police/Sheriff's Department, the State Attorney's Office, or a private attorney.

In Your School. If your school has no sexual harassment policy, take the lead toward getting a policy. Ask other students to help you. Find an adult to advise and support the group.

Be a support person for someone who is being harassed. Having another person who understands can give someone the courage to tell the harasser to stop. If the harassment continues, offer to go with the person to report it.

In Your Community. Help elect candidates who support equal rights. Remember, you may not be able to vote, but you can still do a lot to help and support candidates.

Nationally. Join a national organization that supports equal rights for women. You can join the group or organize a group of your own.

Elections for U.S. Senators and Representatives are a chance to get involved nationally. Help send someone to Congress who will work for women's rights.

❖ FIGHTING SEXISM AROUND ❖ THE WORLD

Women everywhere are working toward equal rights. Sexism has kept women down. All over

the world women are standing up and saying, "You can't do that to us anymore." Almost every country in the world has women's organizations that work for women's rights. They are taking leadership roles in their countries to put an end to sexism, harassment, and sexual discrimination.

There are people from the United States who volunteer to go to other countries to work for human rights. One group that works directly in foreign countries is the Peace Corps. Peace Corps volunteers work hand in hand with the people in a country. They work to help people improve their technical and leadership skills. Helping women in developing countries is an important aspect of Peace Corps volunteer work.

Many international organizations work for women's rights and improving the status of women everywhere. *The Encyclopedia of International Associations* has a list of those groups. There are organizations that monitor changes in law and public policy around the world and encourage cooperation and communication between women of all backgrounds, beliefs, nationalities, and age groups.

❖ THE END OF SEXUAL HARASSMENT ❖ AND SEXISM

Working with others, you can help in the

ongoing fight to end sexual harassment and sexism. Every step you take toward ending sexism is one step further along the road. From 1164, when Héloïse tried to bring education to women in France, until 1993, when a woman first climbed into the pilot's seat of an American jet fighter, the road has been rough. That has not stopped many women, and it shouldn't stop you.

You know what sexual harassment is. You can speak out against it. Don't let your silence give approval to harassers as the admiral's did at the Tailhook Convention. Get together with others to stop sexism and sexual harassment. Take action, now. You *can* make a difference.

❖ QUESTIONS TO ASK YOURSELF ❖

Harassment and sexism are being fought around the world. 1) Do you know what to do if you are harassed? 2) Are you interested in political action in your school and community? 3) Are you interested in helping women in countries around the world fight sexual harassment?

GLOSSARY

AIDS (acquired immunodeficiency syndrome) A fatal sexually transmitted disease.

campaign Activities undertaken to promote a candidate or a cause.

candidate Person running for a political office.

caucus A group of people united to promote a cause.

discrimination The act of prejudging someone based on his or her sex, race, etc., rather than on the basis of qualifications.

feminism Movement that supports equal social and political rights for women.

harassment Bothering repeatedly.

herstory History presented from a feminist viewpoint.

hostile Unfriendly.

human rights Rights that all people possess as human beings.

humanitarian Having concern for the welfare of people.

intern Someone in training for a short time.

intimidate To force people to do something or to not do something because of fear.

Peace Corps United States government agency that sends volunteers to help people in developing countries.

personnel People who work for a business or service provider.

policy Written or agreed-upon course of action toward an objective.

political Having to do with politics or government.

political campaign Activities undertaken by a candidate and her or his followers to win an election.

poll The voting during an election; the place where one votes; a sampling of public opinion.

sexism Discrimination on the basis of sex.

sexual harassment Unwanted and/or unwelcome sexual behavior of any kind toward another person.

social climate Attitude, mood, and spirit of the people in a community.

tract Small printed publication; pamphlet.

violate To degrade or spoil; to go against a rule.

Organizations to Contact

**National Organization
  for Women (NOW)**
1000 16th Street NW
Washington, DC 20036
(202) 331-0066
e-mail: now@now.org

**National Teenage
  Republican
  Headquarters**
P.O. Box 1896
Manassas, VA 22110
(703) 368-4214

**National Women's
  Political Caucus**
12-11 Connecticut Avenue
  NW
Washington, DC 20036
(202) 785-1100
e-mail: mailnwpc@aol.com

**NOW Legal Defense and
  Education Fund**
99 Hudson Street
New York, NY 10013
(212) 925-6635

**United Nations
  Development Fund
  for Women**
304 East 45th Street
New York, NY 10017
(212) 906-6400

**Young Democrats of
  America**
c/o Democratic National
  Committee
430 South Capitol Street
  SE
Washington, DC 20003
(202) 863-8000
e-mail: yda@democrats.org

IN CANADA

Women Plan Toronto
736 Bathurst Street
Toronto, ON M5S 2R4
(416) 588-9751

FOR FURTHER READING

Backhouse, Constance, and Cohen, Leah. *Sexual Harassment on the Job*. Englewood Cliffs, NJ: Prentice-Hall, 1981.

Berger, Gilda. *Women, Wages, and Work*. New York: Franklin Watts, 1986.

Black, Beryl. *Coping with Sexual Harassment*, rev. ed. New York: Rosen Publishing Group, 1990.

Bouchard, Elizabeth. *Everything You Need to Know About Sexual Harassment*. New York: Rosen Publishing Group, 1992.

French, Marilyn. *The War Against Women*. New York: Summit Books, 1992.

Kemmel, Michael S., and Mosmiller, Thomas E. *Against the Tide: Pro-Feminist Men in the U.S. 1776–1990*. Boston, MA: Beacon Press, 1992.

Lewis, Barbara. *The Kids' Guide to Social Action*. Minneapolis, MN: Free Spirit Publishing, 1991.

Morgan, Robin. *Sisterhood Is Global*. Garden City, NY: Anchor Press/Doubleday, 1984.

INDEX

ABOUT THE AUTHOR

Rhoda McFarland has taught all grades, kindergarten through twelfth. She is a certified alcoholism and drug abuse counselor having worked with troubled young people and their parents. She developed and implemented the first educational program in the California area for students making the transition from drug/alcohol treatment programs back into the regular school system. She was a Peace Corps Volunteer in Belize, Central America.

PHOTO CREDITS: Cover photo © A/P Wide World; p. 2 © Image Bank/ Ken Huang; pp. 8, 45 by Yung-Hee Chia; p. 11 © Impact Visuals/Rick Reinhard; p. 13 © Impact Visuals/Bill Burke; p. 17 © A/P Wide World; p. 21 © Impact Visuals/Marilyn Humphries; p. 26 © A/P Wide World; p. 28 by Olga M. Palma; p. 31 © Image Bank/Sumo; pp. 35, 49 by Matthew Baumann/Kim Sonsky; pp. 38, 55 by Kim Sonsky; p. 41 by Michael Brandt.

PHOTO RESEARCH: Vera Amadzadeh

DESIGN: Kim Sonsky